PAT METHENY | ORCHESTRION

Score prepared by Pat Metheny

Assistant - Greg Federico

ISBN 978-1-4234-7603-0

HAL•LEONARD®
CORPORATION
7777 W. BLUEMOUND RD. P.O. BOX 13819 MILWAUKEE, WI 53213

Visit Hal Leonard Online at
www.halleonard.com

THE ORCHESTRION SUITE

Composed by Pat Metheny

1
Orchestrion

(End Guitar Harmonics)

(LAY BACK)

5

ACCENTS

D⁷sus

UNISON

EE

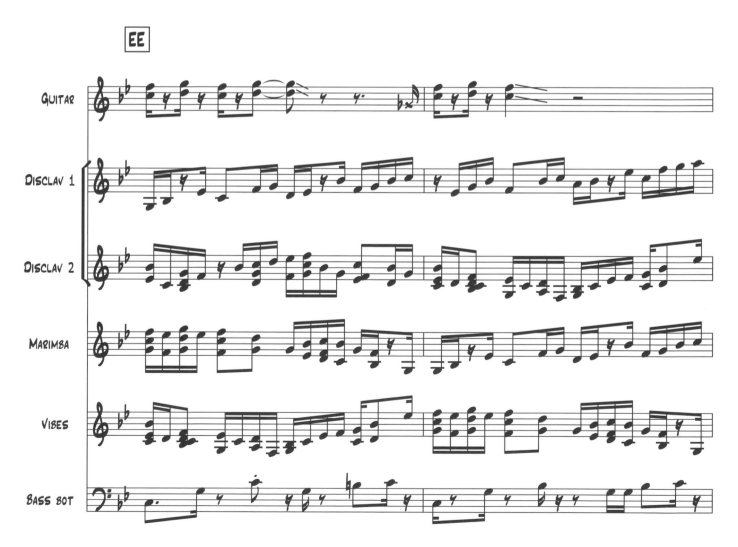

TT SOLO STARTS - GROOVE

CCC

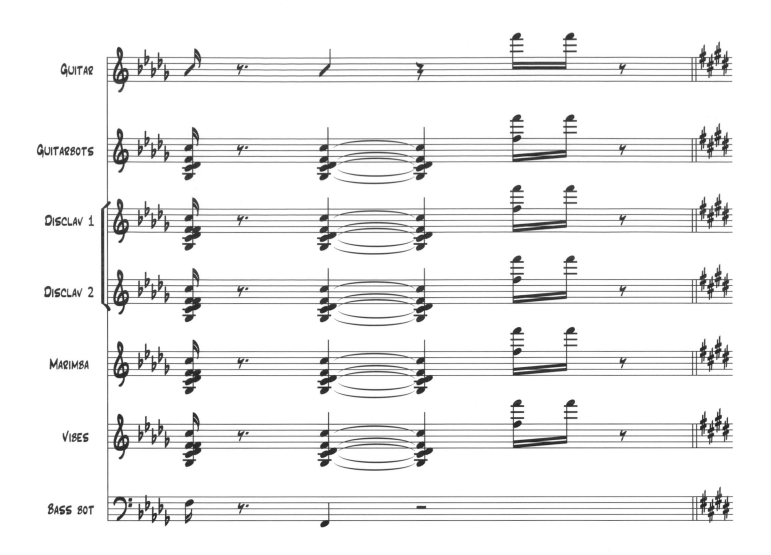

III GROOVE

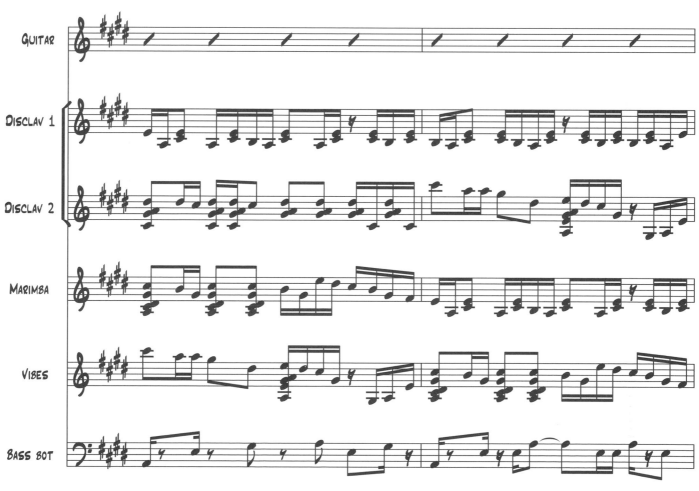

114

118

FFFF

126

Entry Point

By Pat Metheny

Q Guitar Solo

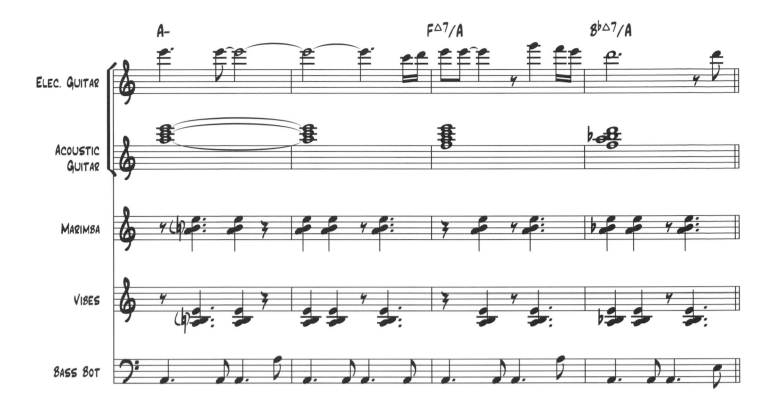

159

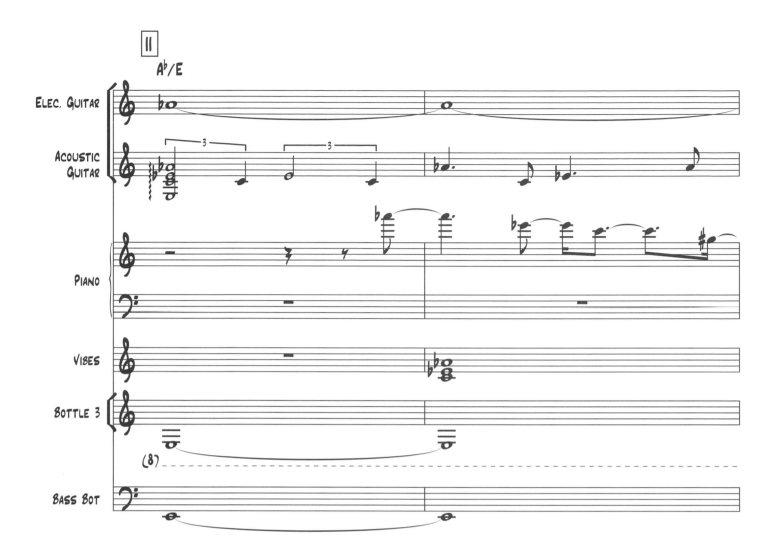

III
Expansion

By Pat Metheny

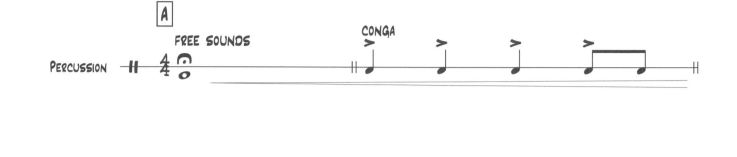

169

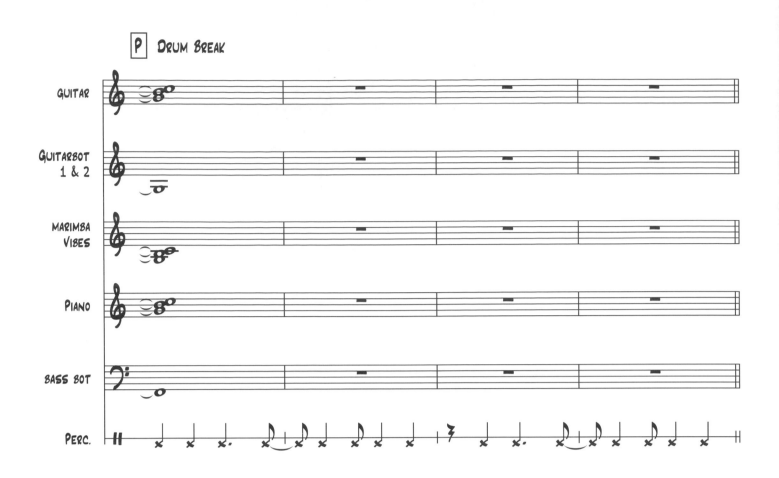

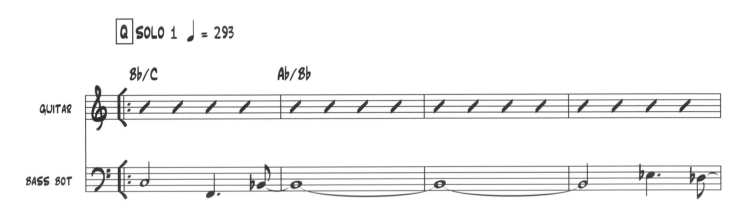

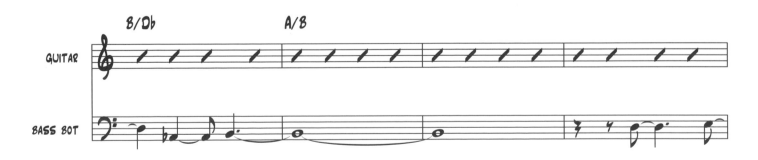

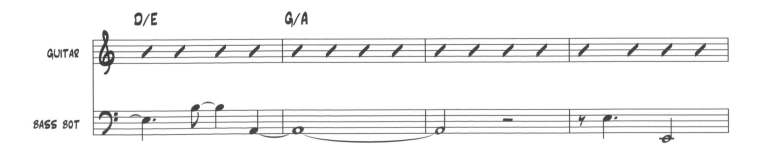

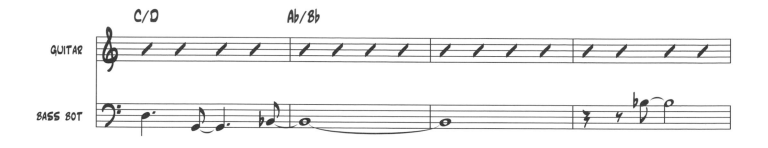

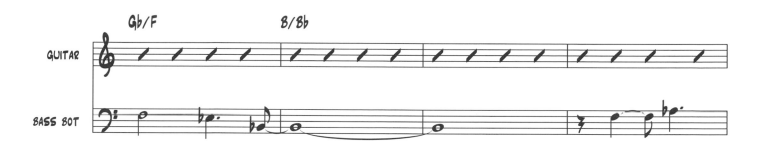

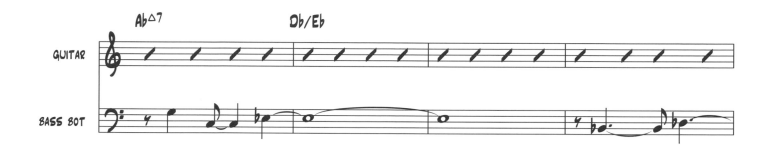

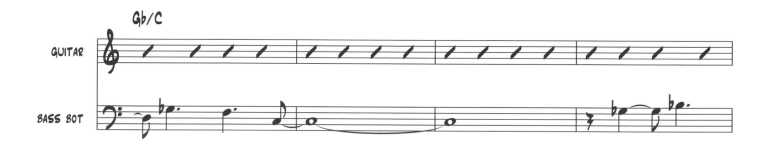

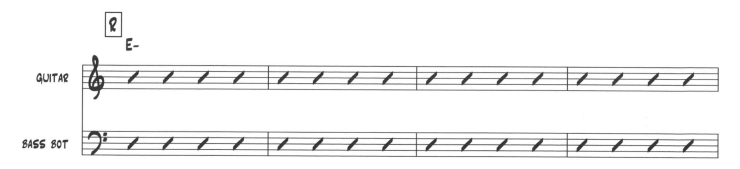

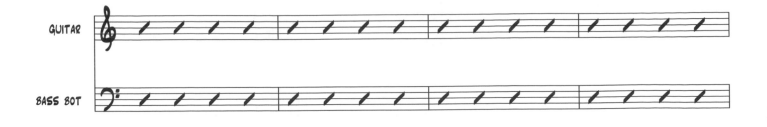

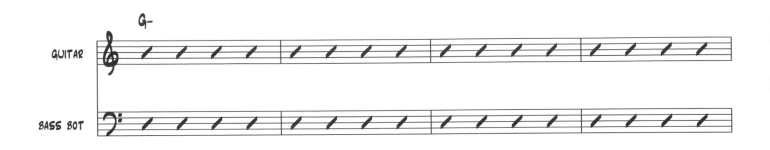

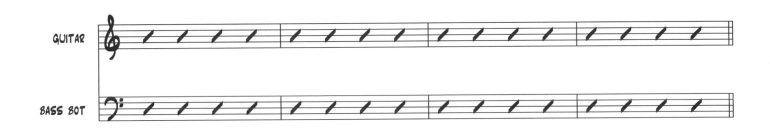

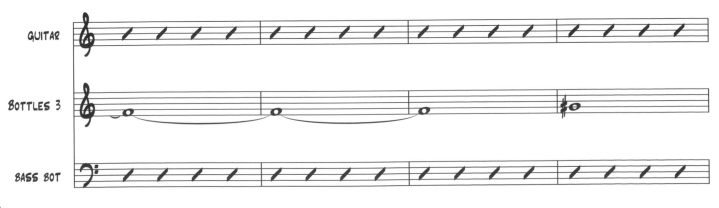

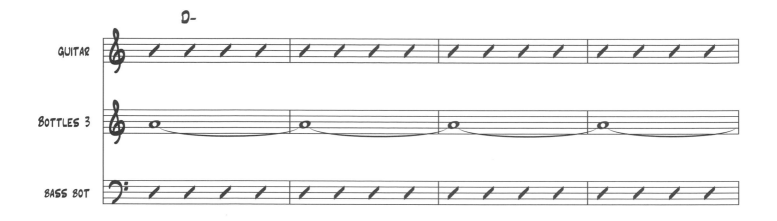

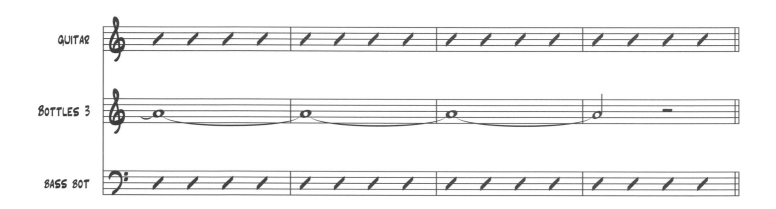

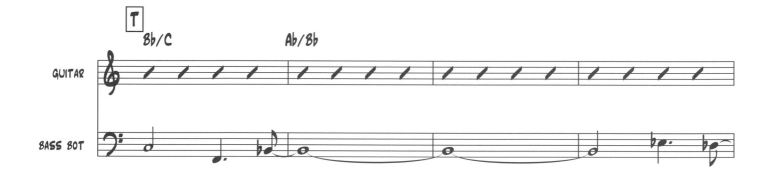

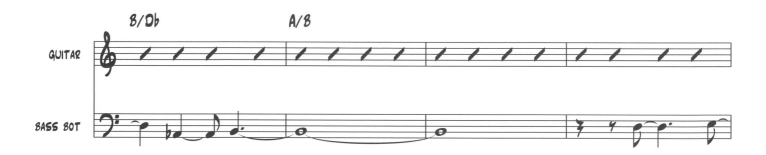

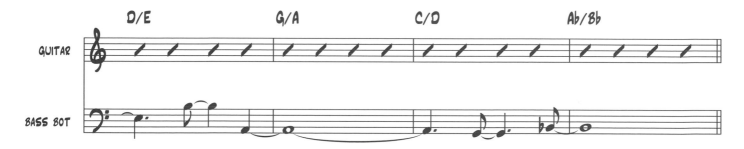

179

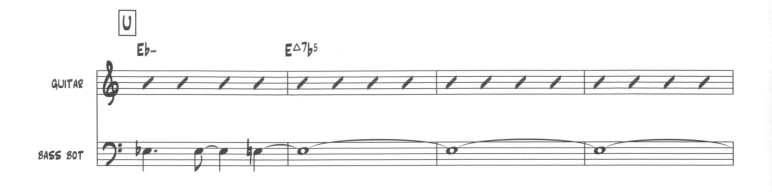

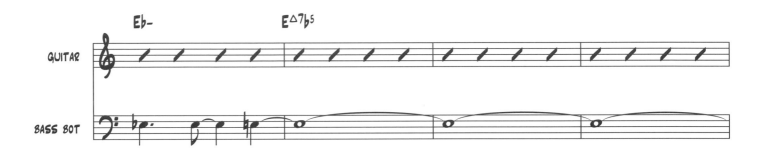

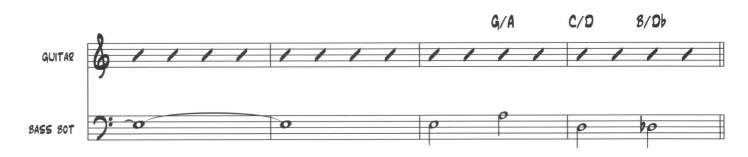

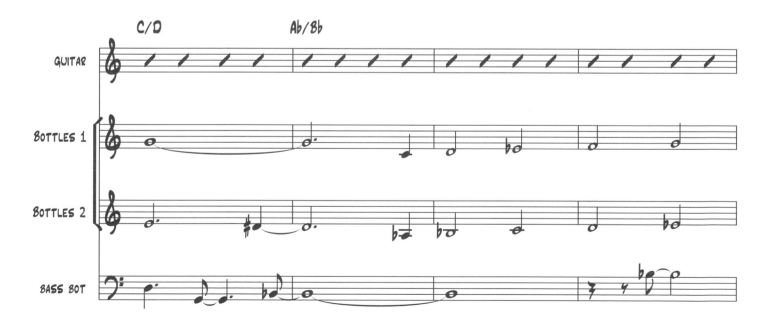

181

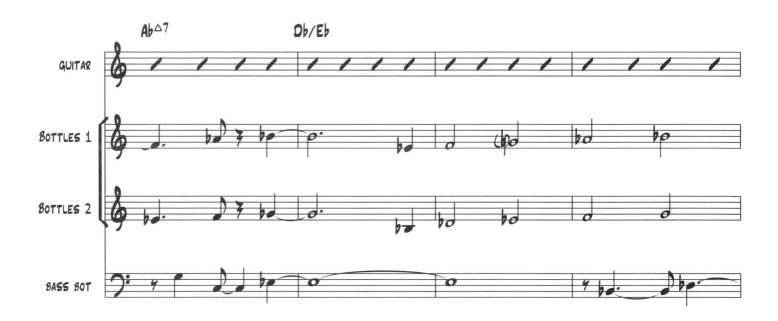

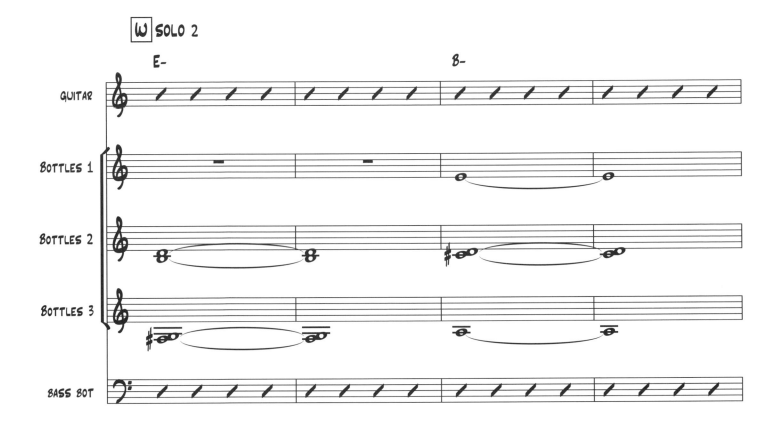

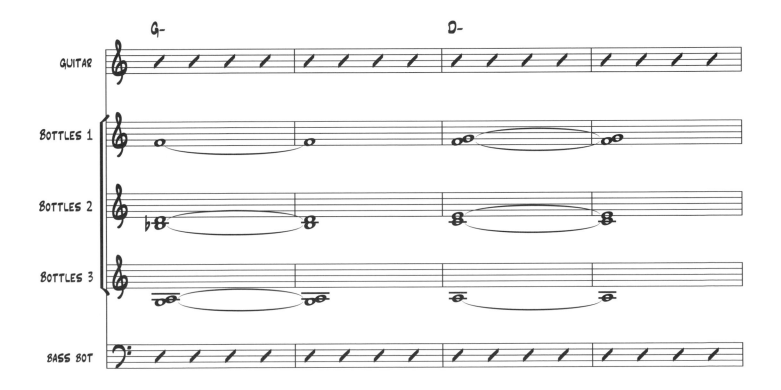

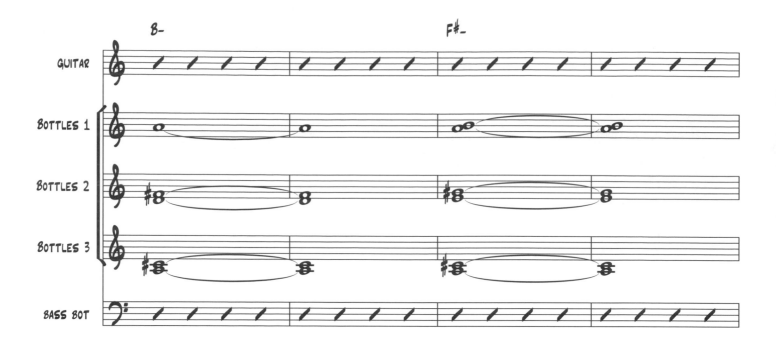

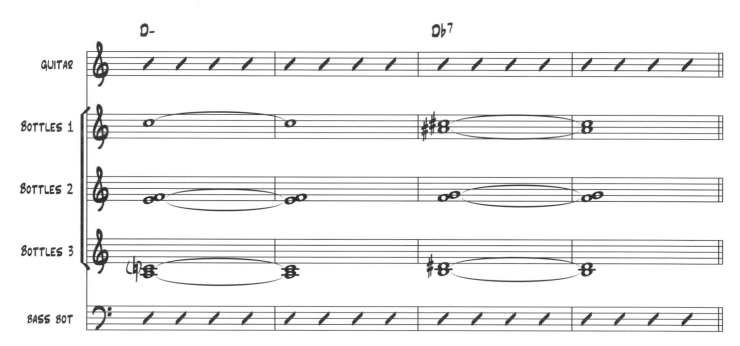

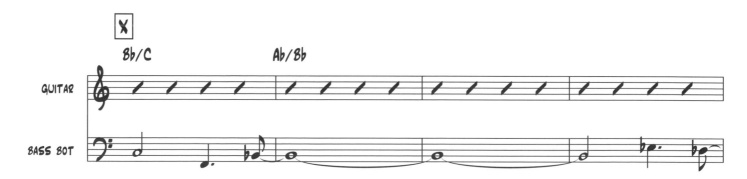

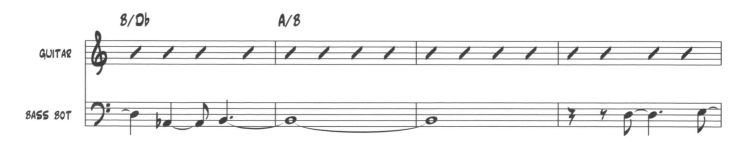

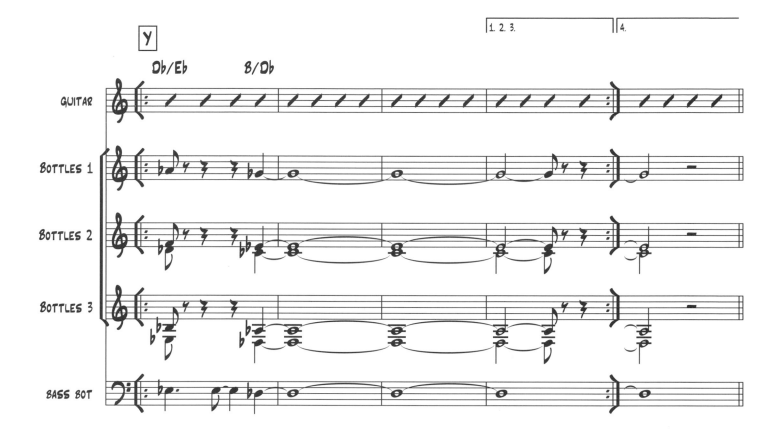

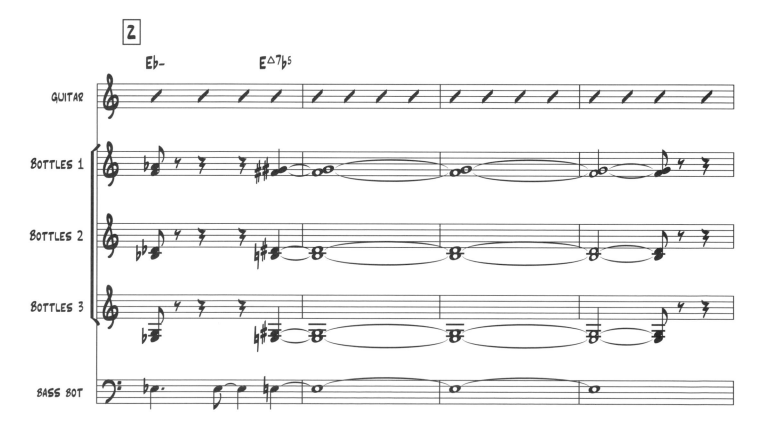

185

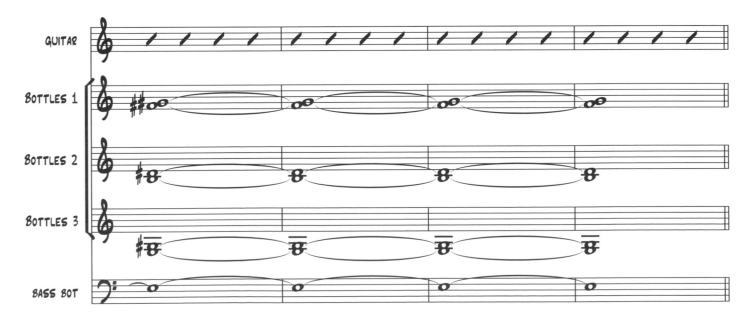

AA ENSEMBLE BREAK

BB ♩ = 155

DRUM BREAK

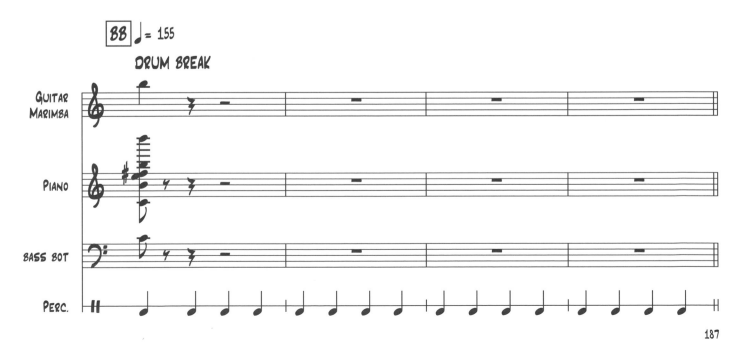

193

IV
Soul Search

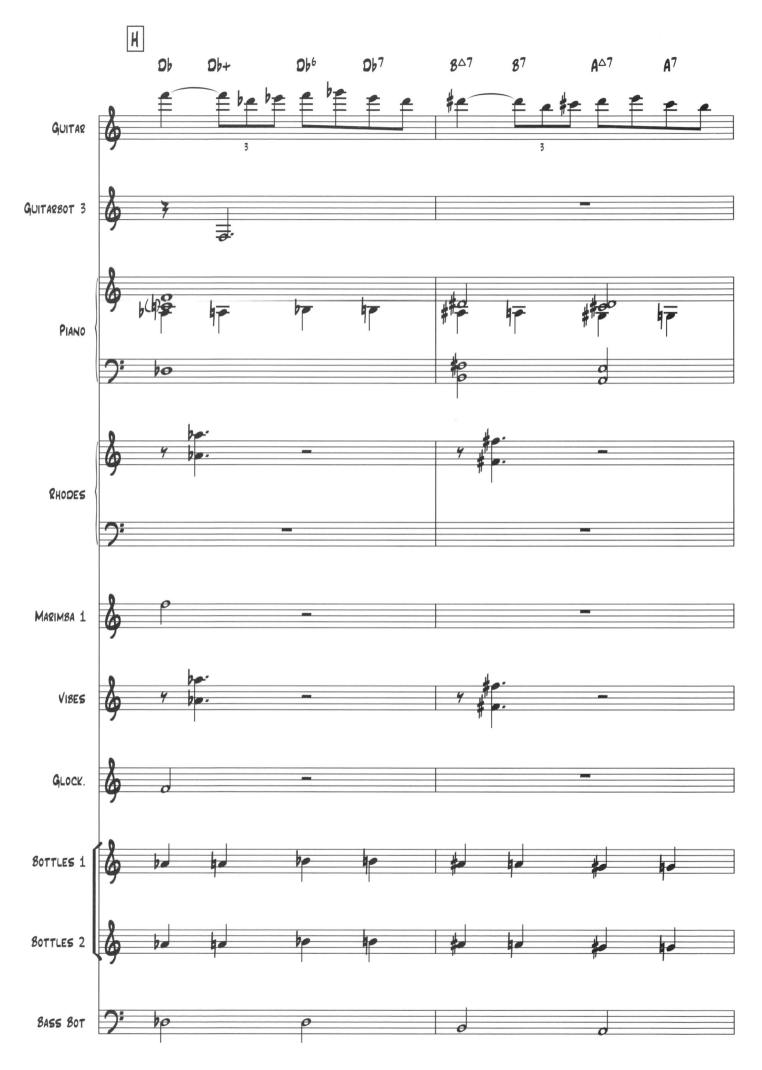

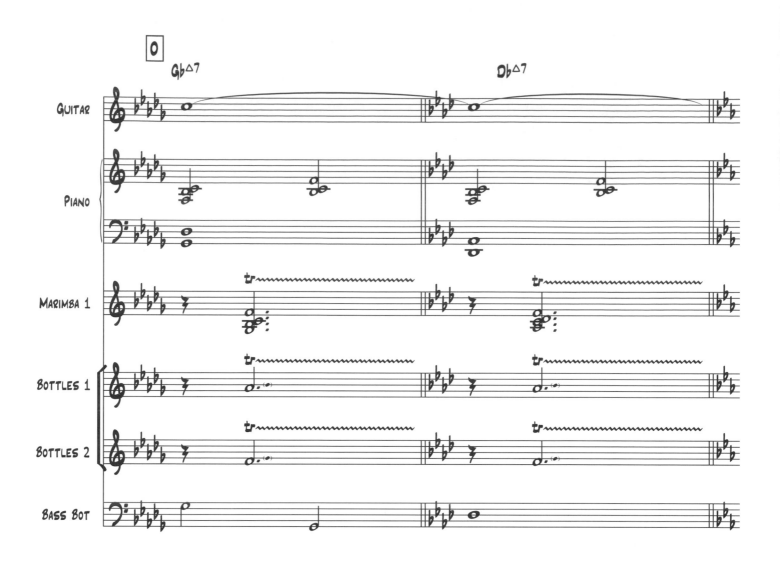

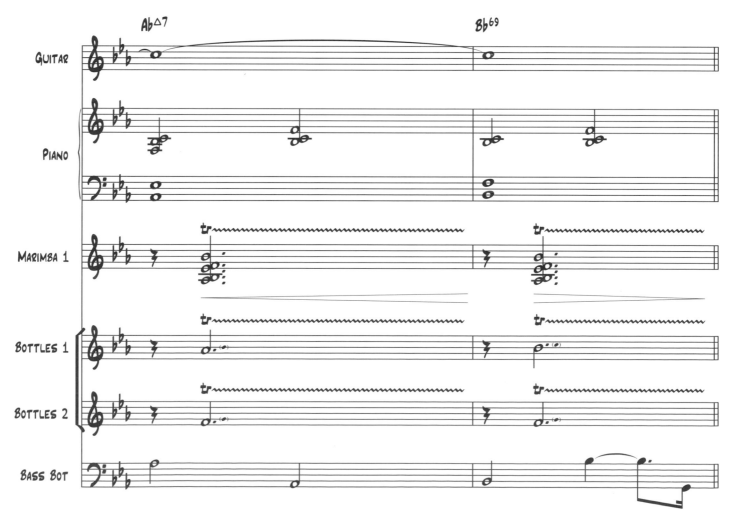

234

V

Spirit of the Air

D **VIBES PART - LOOP THREE**

GUITAR MELODY

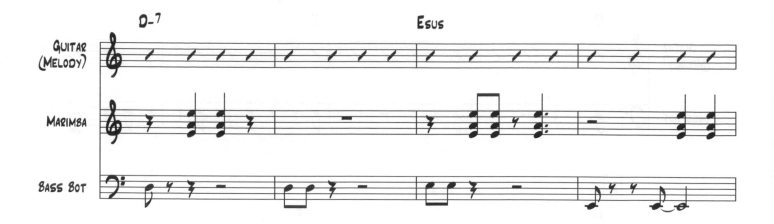